Lyndon B. Johnson

Lyndon B. Johnson

Jean Kinney Williams

AMERICA'S
36TH
PRESIDENT

Children's Press®
A Division of Scholastic Inc.
New York / Toronto / London / Auckland / Sydney
Mexico City / New Delhi / Hong Kong
Danbury, Connecticut

Library of Congress Cataloging-in-Publication Data

Williams, Jean Kinney.
    Lyndon B. Johnson / Jean Kinney Williams.
        p. cm. — (Encyclopedia of presidents. Second series)
        Includes bibliographical references and index.
    ISBN 0-516-22977-X
    1. Johnson, Lyndon B. (Lyndon Baines), 1908–1973—Juvenile literature. 2.
Presidents—United States—Biography—Juvenile literature. 3. United States—
Politics and government—1963–1969—Juvenile literature. I. Title. II.
Encyclopedia of presidents (2003)
E847.W7283 2005
973.923'092—dc22   2004019422

Contents

Chapter 1

A Passion for Politics ——————

According to family legend, on the August morning in 1908 when Lyndon Baines Johnson was born, his grandfather rode through the settlements of the Texas Hill Country announcing, "A United States senator was born this morning!" The story may or may not be true, but Lyndon Johnson enjoyed telling it. Like his Texas tall tales, Johnson often seemed larger than life. He was nearly six feet four inches tall (190 centimeters) with jug-sized ears and big hands that he waved about as he spoke. "He'd come through a door and he'd take the whole room over. Just like that," said his vice president, Hubert Humphrey.

Johnson was a champion persuader. He would put his face within inches of others' to get their attention, jabbing his finger into their chests to drive home his point. During a long career in Congress, he became a master of legislation—turning *bills* (proposed laws) into law. As president, Johnson used those talents to help change American society. The 89th Congress, which met between January 1965 and October 1966, passed nearly 200 bills, most of them with Johnson's active support. Johnson helped pass more important legislation in those two years than many presidents have passed during two four-year terms.

Johnson might be considered one of the great U.S. presidents in history, except that his term of office was darkened by U.S. involvement in the long Vietnam War, which ignited intense and often violent protests at home. His huge successes as a legislator, especially in the area of civil rights, were shadowed by his inability to win or end the war.

Early Life

Johnson was born August 27, 1908, near Stonewall, in the Hill Country of central Texas, about 75 miles (125 kilometers) west of Austin, the state capital. The region's rolling hills and thin soil made it better suited to ranching than to farming. Even though enterprising men had made fortunes grazing cattle there, the region was sparsely populated and many of its residents were poor. Lyndon Johnson spent most of his adult life in Washington, D.C., but he remained deeply attached to the rugged land of his childhood.

Johnson was born in this small frame house, which stood a quarter mile (0.4 km) from the later LBJ Ranch. The house was torn down in the 1940s, but a replica has been built on the original site and is open to visitors.

Johnson's parents were Sam Ealy Johnson Jr., and Rebekah Baines Johnson. The Johnsons had long connections to the Hill Country. Lyndon's grandfather, Sam Ealy Sr., had made a fortune there as a rancher in the 1870s. He raised cattle in the Hill Country, then drove them overland to Kansas City for sale. He later lost most of his money when cattle prices plunged. One of Sam's nephews laid out the nearby town of Johnson City in 1879. Lyndon's father, Sam Ealy Jr., was born in the Hill Country in 1877. Soon after Lyndon's birth, he moved the family to a farm near Johnson City, where he struggled to make a living as he became a politician, serving several terms in the Texas legislature.

On his mother's side, one of Lyndon's great-great-uncles was John Wheeler Bunton, a signer of the Texas Declaration of Independence in 1836, and a contributor to the constitution of the new Republic of Texas. Lyndon's grandfather, Joseph Wilson Baines, had served as Texas secretary of state.

Lyndon's mother, Rebekah Johnson, was educated and interested in culture, but often felt overwhelmed by conditions on the family's modest farm, where she raised her five children. There was no electricity, gas, or indoor plumbing to help with chores like cooking, washing clothes, and growing and canning the family's garden produce. She poured her love of literature into firstborn Lyndon, who could recite poetry by age three. By age four he was attending the small schoolhouse nearby.

Lyndon Johnson's parents, Rebekah Johnson and Sam Ealy Johnson Jr.

As a boy Lyndon relished the time he spent with his father as Sam cam-

paigned for office. As they drove the Hill Country back roads, stopping to talk to

farmers working in the fields, Lyndon learned from his father's friendly campaign

style. Sam chatted about crops or local gossip, then mentioned his work in the

state legislature in Austin. Later, Lyndon practiced his father's folksy manners when he shined shoes at the Johnson City barbershop. After reading the day's newspaper, he would talk about current events with his customers.

When Lyndon was a teenager, Sam Johnson lost the family farm when the price of cotton fell from 40 cents per pound to 8 cents. The family struggled to get by on Sam's small income as a state legislator. When Lyndon graduated from high school in 1924, he showed little interest in finding a career. He traveled to California, then went to work on a road-building crew with some of his friends. One man in Johnson City said of Sam Johnson's family, "None of them will ever amount to a damn."

Soon Johnson quit the road-building crew. "I'm sick of working with just my hands," he told his mother. He was ready, he said, to "make it with my brain."

College Days

In March 1927, 18-year-old Lyndon Johnson arrived at Southwest Texas State Teachers College in San Marcos, about 50 miles (80 km) from home. Southwest was not a selective college, but Johnson was not well enough prepared to gain admission to a better school. The college also offered low tuition and living expenses. Johnson studied history, planning to become a teacher. He also got involved in journalism and debating. To pay his expenses he worked as a garbage collector and janitor. Later he convinced the college president, who knew

The children of Sam and Rebekah Johnson: Lucia, Josefa, Rebekah, Lyndon (age 13), and Sam Jr.

Lyndon's father, to hire him as an office assistant. It was the first of many times that Johnson would seek out the support of a helpful older mentor.

After three terms at Southwest, Johnson took a year off to work as a teacher in Cotulla, a small impoverished town only 60 (96 km) miles from the

When Lyndon Johnson arrived at Welhausen School in dusty little Cotulla, Texas, he saw that many of his students lived in rickety shacks. He also learned that many families had little to eat. The school had no lunch period, because so many of its students had no lunches. This degree of poverty was new to Johnson, but it didn't discourage him from urging his students forward.

He convinced the school board to buy Welhausen School volleyballs, softballs, and bats, which the town's "Anglo" school already had. He ran a strict classroom and insisted that his students speak English, which he believed would help them succeed in American society. He held spelling bees and trained his students to compete with other schools in debate. He organized track meets and softball games, the first after-school activities for Welhausen students. Years later, Johnson said that he could "still see the faces of the children who sat in my class" in Cotulla.

Johnson, 21 years old, with fellow teachers in an elementary school in Cotulla, Texas. His experiences that year with needy students began a life-long interest in improving education.

When Johnson later supported free school lunch programs, better teachers' salaries, and the Head Start program for preschoolers, he still had his Cotulla students in mind. Providing an education for all American children had become one of his missions in life.

☆ ☆ ☆

Mexican border. Most of the students at the school were children of Mexican immigrants. Though his students were poorly prepared, Johnson took his job seriously and let them know he had high expectations for them. Johnson first encountered severe poverty in Cotulla, and he never forgot the trials and the successes of his students there.

In the fall of 1929, Johnson returned to San Marcos and pushed hard to finish college. He also jumped into college politics, running a slate of less-popular students for the student government. Like his father, Lyndon practiced one-on-one campaigning. With Lyndon's help his friend was able to beat the campus football star for student body president by eight votes.

High School Teacher

Johnson finished college in 1930. The Great Depression was just beginning, and unemployment was already widespread. Johnson was lucky to find a job as a teacher at Sam Houston High School in Houston, through his uncle George Johnson, who was already a teacher there. Lyndon was hired to teach speech, geography, and mathematics. He promised school officials that the Sam Houston debate team would win the city championship the next spring. He taught his young debaters the same skills that he was developing to master politics. Explaining how to approach debate judges, Johnson said, "Act like you're talking to those folks. Look one of them in the eye, then move on and look another one in the eye." The team won the city championship and placed second in the state of Texas.

The school wanted Johnson to return the next year, but he had learned that he wasn't satisfied with teaching. When Johnson visited Austin that year to lobby lawmakers for better teachers' pay, Congressman-elect Richard Kleberg offered him a job as his office aide in Washington. Johnson accepted the offer, which would mean leaving Texas for life in Washington, D.C. Lyndon Johnson had found his true calling.

Chapter 2

Assistant in Washington ————————

According to Johnson biographer Robert Dallek, Lyndon Johnson developed a burning desire "to be the best, to outdo friend and foe." He had already demonstrated it in college politics and in teaching. Now this powerful competitive instinct would have plenty of room to grow in Washington, D.C. Arriving there in December 1931, he lived in an inexpensive hotel with other young government employees. Before he even finished unpacking, he was roaming the halls of the hotel, introducing himself. Talking politics became his passion. A roommate recalled that Johnson "couldn't have cared less" for other activities, such as going to a movie or a baseball game with friends.

In Congress, Johnson sought out leaders of the Texas delegation. One in particular became a longtime mentor and friend. Sam Rayburn had worked with Lyndon's father in the Texas legislature,

Representative Sam Rayburn was Lyndon Johnson's political mentor in Washington. Rayburn served in the House from 1913 to 1961, and was Speaker of the House for 17 years between 1941 and 1961.

and had represented an East Texas district in Congress since 1912. By 1932 Rayburn was a powerful committee chairman, and later he would serve as Speaker of the House for 17 years. Rayburn remained a close friend and adviser to Johnson for nearly 30 years.

Representative Kleberg, Johnson's boss, was a wealthy Texas rancher and showed little interest in the day-to-day business of Congress. Soon young Lyndon Johnson was running his office. In 1932, Johnson worked as Kleberg's campaign manager and helped him win re-election to the House. Another congressional aide recalled that Johnson knew in a matter of months "how to operate in Washington better than some who had been here 20 years."

The 1932 election was a major turning point for the country and for Democrats in Congress. The economic depression had gotten worse, and now millions were unemployed. Many were homeless and hungry. In the presidential election, Democrat Franklin D. Roosevelt promised a "New Deal"—prompt government action to help the needy and end hard times. Roosevelt was elected by a landslide, and dozens of new Democrats were elected to Congress.

As Kleberg's office manager, Johnson learned firsthand how to be a congressman. He answered mail from *constituents*, the people in Kleberg's district, and returned to Texas to meet with voters. Kleberg, a conservative Democrat, was not inclined to vote for Roosevelt's New Deal programs. Johnson, on the other hand, was an enthusiastic Roosevelt supporter. He knew that the people of Texas were suffering with the rest of the nation and advised Kleberg to support the New Deal. Once he even threatened to resign if Kleberg voted against a bill to boost farm prices for struggling farmers.

Johnson also began preparing for a career in politics himself. In 1934 he enrolled at Georgetown University Law School, hoping to get a law degree, which might help him win future elections. He had never been an enthusiastic student, though, and he soon grew impatient with classes and dropped out. He would pursue his political career without a law degree.

Lady Bird ───────────────────────────

In the summer of 1934, while visiting in Texas, Johnson met Claudia Taylor, a young woman in her early 20s. Nicknamed "Lady Bird" by her nursemaid as an infant, she was the daughter of a wealthy businessman. Her mother died when

Claudia Taylor was nicknamed "Lady Bird" as a child. Intelligent but shy, she studied history and journalism at the University of Texas. She and Lyndon Johnson were married in 1934.

Lady Bird was only five, and she was raised by an aunt whose love of culture and nature Lady Bird came to share. She graduated from the University of Texas, where she studied journalism to help conquer her shyness.

Lady Bird was enthralled by the bold and outgoing congressional assistant. Johnson liked Lady Bird well enough to propose marriage on their first date. After a whirlwind courtship, they eloped on November 17, 1934, just three months later. Calm and agreeable, Lady Bird provided a stark contrast to Lyndon's often over-bearing behavior. She would not enjoy an easy marriage, but they remained deeply devoted to each other until his death in 1973.

By 1935 disagreements between Johnson and Congressman Kleberg cost Johnson his job, but he already had his eye on a challenging new assignment. Through his close friendship with Sam Rayburn, Johnson was appointed Texas director of a New Deal jobs program, the National Youth Administration (NYA). As Johnson and Lady Bird packed to return to Texas, Lyndon had some parting words for his Washington friends: "When I come back to Washington, I'm coming back as a congressman."

Return to Texas

The Johnsons moved to Austin, where Lyndon set up the new NYA offices, hiring old friends from high school and college to help him. The NYA program

JOBS

GET THE FACTS
ABOUT OCCUPATIONS

Free Classes
... for ...

YOUNG MEN AND WOMEN 16 TO 25 YRS.

NATIONAL YOUTH ADMINISTRATION of ILLINOIS
WILLIAM J. CAMPBELL ... STATE DIRECTOR

FEDERAL ART PROJECT·WPA·ILL.

A poster of the National Youth Administration advertising free classes.
Lyndon Johnson was the director of the NYA in Texas.

enrolled young people of high school and college age, paying them for part-time work as clerks or janitors. The small salaries they received made it possible for them to stay in school and often helped their struggling families. The program reached thousands in the state, including Mexican Americans and African Americans, who faced much discrimination in the job force.

Among their many accomplishments, NYA members in Texas built small parks along state highways and helped restore the historic center of San Antonio, near the Alamo, which became popular with tourists. More than 30,000 young Texans worked for the NYA. Even though Johnson was the youngest NYA administrator in the country, he became one of the most successful. The program reinforced his growing belief that government could help change people's lives for the better. He also realized that 30,000 young

Texans earning much-appreciated paychecks could offer valuable political support in future elections.

In February 1937, the representative of Texas's 10th Congressional District, which included Austin and Johnson City, died in office. Several local Democrats were eager to run for the vacant seat, but Johnson, now 28 years old, was at the front of the line. Lady Bird took $10,000 from a trust fund established for her by her father to help finance her husband's campaign.

Johnson ran on his experience as a congressional aide in Washington and on his enthusiastic support for the New Deal. "A VOTE FOR JOHNSON IS A VOTE FOR ROOSEVELT'S PROGRAMS," read one of his campaign banners. Following his father's lead, Johnson drove through the district to meet voters personally. Two days before the election, Johnson was rushed to the hospital with appendicitis, and his appendix was removed. He recovered from the operation in time to hear the election results in his hospital bed. He had won by more than 3,000 votes.

Soon after the election, Johnson was invited to meet President Roosevelt, who was vacationing in Galveston, Texas. Roosevelt congratulated the young congressman and encouraged him to try for a seat on the Naval Affairs Committee in Congress. The president said that Europe appeared headed for war, and he would need support in Congress to equip U.S. military forces. Back in

Soon after his election to Congress, Johnson (right) meets President Franklin Roosevelt (left) in Galveston, Texas. The two were introduced by Texas governor James Allred (center).

Washington, Roosevelt told a White House aide, "I've just met the most remarkable young man. Help him with anything you can."

Before leaving for Washington, Johnson visited his father, who would die later that year. Sam Johnson told his son, "Measure each vote you cast by this standard: Is this vote in the benefit of the people? What does it do for human beings? . . . Now, you get up there, support FDR all the way, never shimmy, and give 'em hell!"

Youngest Congressman

Now the youngest member of the House, Johnson hired two friends as office aides. As he would do for the rest of his life, Johnson worked around the clock and expected his assistants to do the same. Many could not keep pace, resigning when they were completely exhausted. Lady Bird had her jobs, too, including taking visitors from the 10th District on tours of Washington. "Lyndon was always prodding me to . . . learn more, work harder. . . . It is really very stimulating. It is also very tiring," she said later.

Johnson knew that the harder he worked for his district, the better his political career would go. He got government money to improve roads in his district, which provided valuable jobs for his constituents. Later, he helped bring an experimental low-income housing project to Austin. He became a strong supporter of a program that would bring electricity to remote areas like the Texas Hill Country. When electric power arrived in rural regions, it revolutionized farm life. Some families were so grateful that they named children for the political leaders who brought electricity to their farms.

Johnson also formed close relationships with businessmen in his district. For example, the firm of Brown & Root received major contracts for construction of a dam in Texas and for building transmission lines for rural electrification. The owners, brothers Herman and George Brown, remained loyal Johnson supporters and grew wealthy carrying out major construction projects for the government. As Johnson saw it, helping Texas businesses meant jobs for his constituents and helped his own career. He was careful, however, not to be too closely tied to wealthy supporters, especially in the oil business. Any suggestion that he profited personally from their success could sink his political future.

On September 1, 1939, the armies of Nazi Germany invaded Poland, beginning World War II. By mid-1940, German troops occupied much of western Europe. The war caused great concern in the United States. It persuaded Democrats to nominate Franklin Roosevelt for a third term, arguing that his strong hand was needed to deal with this world crisis.

The Democratic party was scrambling for campaign money, however. Lyndon Johnson volunteered to direct a special three-week campaign for the Democratic National Committee. In this brief time, Johnson worked frantically to raise the desperately needed funds from wealthy Democratic supporters across the country. He raised the money and funneled it to the close races where it would make the most difference. On election day, Roosevelt was re-elected, and Johnson was elected to his second full term. Thanks in part to Johnson's fund-raising, Democrats also gained additional seats in the House of Representatives.

Johnson's contribution to victory gained him the gratitude of his party, but when he returned to the House early in 1941, the work was a letdown after the

Johnson and Speaker Sam Rayburn during a meeting in Texas.

campaign season whirlwind. That spring, Texas senator Morris Sheppard died. With Roosevelt's support, Johnson announced his candidacy for the Senate seat. Since there were few Republicans in Texas, his only serious rival was Democratic governor "Pappy" O'Daniel, a self-made millionaire who had gained popularity through his entertaining radio broadcasts. In the Democratic primary, Johnson and O'Daniel finished far ahead of 27 other candidates, but neither claimed a majority, so they faced a runoff election in August. Before the polls closed on the day of the runoff, Johnson made a critical mistake. He announced that he was ahead of O'Daniel and revealed how many votes he was leading by. That information was all O'Daniel's men needed to know. Before the counting ended, they "found" just enough votes to defeat Johnson. O'Daniel was elected, and Johnson learned a painful lesson.

Wartime Service

Johnson returned to his seat in the House, but didn't have much time to brood over his disappointment. On December 7, 1941, Japanese planes attacked the U.S. naval base at Pearl Harbor, Hawaii. Within days, the United States declared war on Japan, Germany, and Italy. Johnson had promised that if war broke out, he would be among the first to enlist.

Already a member of the U.S. Naval Reserve, Johnson was the first congressman to volunteer for active duty. In the spring of 1942, he was ordered to visit U.S. troops in Australia to report on their readiness for combat against Japan. During his tour, he flew along on a bombing raid against a Japanese position. The plane was hit by anti-aircraft fire and badly damaged, but managed to limp back to base. According to the plane's tail gunner, Johnson was "cool as ice" during the ordeal. In later years, Johnson told dramatic versions of the story, often exaggerating his own role. That flight turned out to be his only combat experience. In June 1942, President Roosevelt ordered all members of Congress to return from military service, and Johnson was soon back in Washington, his military service at an end.

Johnson took a leave of absence from Congress to serve in the U.S. Navy after the United States entered World War II. Soon afterward, President Roosevelt summoned all members of Congress to return to their legislative duties in Washington.

The next few years were frustrating for Johnson. He realized that advancement in the House was slow and uncertain, and he began to cast about for other challenges. Back in Texas, he encouraged Lady Bird to buy a small, struggling radio station, KTBC, in Austin. Lady Bird ran the station, and Johnson helped gain permissions from the Federal Communications Commission to increase the station's broadcast power to reach a larger market. In 1952 the company would add a television station, and its success eventually made the Johnsons wealthy. During these years the Johnsons also became the parents of two daughters. Lynda Bird was born in 1944 and Luci Baines in 1947.

In 1944, with the war still raging, Roosevelt was elected to a fourth term as president. By the time his term began in January 1945, however, he was seriously ill.

In April 1945, he died. Vice President Harry Truman, a former senator from Missouri, was sworn in as president. Johnson grieved the loss of President Roosevelt, who had been a special mentor and friend.

Cold War Politics ———————————————————

Even as World War II was ending, a new "cold war" was beginning. The Soviet Union had been one of the Allied powers fighting Germany. Yet this huge Communist state, made up of present-day Russia and a group of smaller "Socialist Republics," now seemed unwilling to cooperate with other allies and began to create new Communist states in Eastern Europe and Asia. Many American political leaders were suspicious of the Soviets, the only nation in the world that could compete economically and militarily with the United States.

In 1947 President Truman announced the Truman Doctrine, a policy pledging U.S. assistance to countries threatened by Communist aggression. Johnson supported the president and defended the Truman Doctrine in the House. "The one thing a bully fully understands is force," he said. "We have fought two world wars because of our failure to take a position in time."

Back in Texas, Johnson was being challenged by conservative Democrats, who considered him too committed to Roosevelt's programs and policies. When President Truman proposed new *civil rights* laws to ensure voting rights for

House Speaker Rayburn and Johnson (left) supported President Truman (seated) on foreign affairs, but as Southerners, they refused to support his efforts to protect the rights of African Americans.

African Americans, conservative Texans were horrified. Johnson reflected his state's Southern views by voting against Truman's proposals. On another issue, he broke with the Truman administration by voting in favor of the Taft-Hartley Act, which limited the powers of labor unions. Johnson's liberal supporters felt betrayed, but his business friends in Texas were relieved to see he wasn't as liberal as everyone had thought. Johnson's days as a New Deal Democrat were behind him.

By 1948, Texas senator Pappy O'Daniel had become so unpopular that he announced he would not run for another term. At first, Johnson was hesitant to run again, fearing the sting of another defeat. Then a former NYA staff member visited Johnson and reminded him that he had inspired many young Texans to work hard for good government. Johnson shook off his reluctance and announced his candidacy for the Senate. This time, he wouldn't give the election away.

Chapter 3

Another Runoff

Now that Pappy O'Daniel was out of the Senate race, the most popular Democrat in Texas stepped up. Coke Stevenson, who had been an effective and widely respected governor, would give Johnson a tough fight for the Senate. Johnson kicked off his campaign with a rally in Austin, the state capital, but it received little publicity. Johnson's aide John Connally Jr. suggested he campaign across the state using a helicopter. A rare sight at the time, a helicopter would draw attention all by itself. In addition, it allowed Johnson to travel quickly across the huge state, making stops almost anywhere.

Once again, the Democratic primary attracted a large field of candidates. When the votes were tallied, Stevenson and Johnson finished first and second with 40 percent and 34 percent of the votes. Since neither had a majority, they met a few weeks later in a

In 1948 Johnson campaigned through Texas in a helicopter for election to the U.S. Senate. The helicopter, then a rare sight, helped attract attention to his candidacy.

runoff election. This time, out of nearly a million votes cast, Johnson defeated Stevenson by a tiny margin of 87 votes. Stevenson contested the results, claiming that Johnson had "stolen" the election, much as Pappy O'Daniel had "stolen" it in 1941. Certain districts known to favor Johnson reported suspiciously high numbers of votes in his favor. Party officials declared Johnson the winner anyway, and for years afterward, his Texas opponents sarcastically referred to him as "Landslide Lyndon." Since there were so few Republicans in Texas, he easily won the general election and took his seat in the Senate.

Once again, Johnson sought out a powerful, older colleague to teach him the ropes and hasten his advancement. Georgia senator Richard Russell was the leader of conservative Southern senators and a powerful member of the Senate Armed Services Committee, to which Johnson was assigned. Russell, a bachelor, spent much time at the Johnson household and helped the young senator establish himself with the "Southern bloc" of senators, many of whom were chairmen of key committees.

During Johnson's first Senate term, he supported the conservative positions held by the Southern bloc. It opposed demands by President Truman for civil rights laws that would regulate voting in Southern states, allowing African Americans to register and vote. Even though Johnson had been elected with the support of liberals and Texas's few black voters, he continued to oppose Truman's civil rights proposals.

Johnson also stepped up his support for Texas's powerful gas and oil industries. In 1949 they *lobbied* (tried to persuade legislators) to end government regulations that kept them from raising prices of gasoline and oil. Johnson realized his working-class constituents would suffer if prices went up, but in the end he voted in favor of reduced regulation. Johnson then went a step further in protecting the energy companies. When President Truman nominated Leland Olds, a strong critic of gas and oil interests, as a member of the Federal Power Commission, Johnson helped engineer the Senate's rejection of the nomination. During a public committee hearing, he aggressively questioned Olds, suggesting that he was an anti-business radical, perhaps even a Communist. Using narrow, lawyerly questions, he forced Olds into contradicting himself. In the end, the Senate defeated the nomination.

International Crises ──────────────────

International events also required the Senate's attention during Johnson's first year. In 1949 the United States, Canada, and several European nations formed the North Atlantic Treaty Organization (NATO), pledging to defend one another against aggression by Communist states in Europe or North America. That same year, after a long civil war, the Communist party took over China, the most populous country on Earth. The country's anti-Communist opponents fled to the island of Taiwan. The threat of Communism became a matter of grave concern.

In June 1950, the Korean War broke out when forces from the Communist state of North Korea attacked South Korea, a U.S. ally. President Truman persuaded the United Nations to commit to helping South Korea. Most of the troops sent to fight for South Korea were from the United States. In the Senate, Richard Russell appointed Johnson to a newly formed Senate subcommittee that would oversee American war efforts in Korea, putting Johnson in a position to help make military policy. Johnson's committee leadership was praised, and he began gaining national attention.

Fast Facts
KOREAN WAR

Who: North and South Korea; South Korea was aided by United Nations forces, made up largely of Americans; North Korea was aided by China and the Soviet Union.

When: North Korea invaded South Korea in June 1950. The fighting ended after an armistice was signed in July 1953.

Why: Korea was occupied by Japan before and during World War II. In 1945, Soviet and U.S. representatives helped organize northern and southern sectors of Korea. When the two sectors could not agree on plans for a unified Korean government, Communist forces from the North invaded the South, seeking to unify the country by force.

Where: The Korean peninsula, bordered by the Sea of Japan to the east, and China and Russia to the north and northeast

Outcome: Fighting raged over the full length of the Korean peninsula, causing heavy damage and loss of life. The armistice of 1953 set the boundary between North and South near where they had been before, along the 38th parallel. South and North Korea never signed a peace treaty, and relations between them remained tense for more than 50 years.

U.S. troops in combat in Korea during the winter of 1950.

Senate Leader ———————————————

In 1951 Senate Democrats elected Johnson party whip, their second-highest leadership position. It was an honor for a senator who had served only three years, and was a tribute to Johnson's talents and his skill at cultivating powerful senators.

In the 1952 presidential election, Republican Dwight D. Eisenhower was elected, ending 20 years of Democratic rule. Eisenhower, who had commanded Allied forces in Europe during World War II, was popular across the country, even carrying the Democratic stronghold of Texas. Republicans also held on to a thin majority in the Senate, leaving Democrats in the minority. In January 1953, Democrats chose Johnson to their top leadership position in the Senate, minority leader.

A major concern in the Senate during that term was the crusade of Republican senator Joseph McCarthy to find Communists in the government, labor unions, and the entertainment industry. It gradually became clear that McCarthy had little or no real evidence of Communist activity, but he ordered witnesses to testify and was willing to ruin their reputations if they refused to cooperate. Many Democrats in the Senate privately condemned McCarthy's methods, but they were reluctant to speak publicly, since McCarthy might make them targets of his investigations.

In January 1954, McCarthy attacked a highly respected army general with charges of "coddling Communists." In response, the army revealed that McCarthy and his aides had used threats to gain special treatment for a friend who had been drafted into the army. The Senate moved to investigate the charges. Johnson used his influence to persuade television networks to televise the hearings. He believed that when Americans saw McCarthy's bullying tactics for themselves, he would lose public support. Johnson's instincts proved to be correct. Later that year, McCarthy was *censured* (formally condemned) by a vote of three-fourths of the Senate. His power was broken, and his investigations ended.

Majority Leader

In the 1954 congressional elections, Lyndon Johnson was elected to a second six-year term and Democrats regained a majority in the Senate. In January 1955, he was unanimously elected Democratic majority leader, becoming the youngest majority leader in Senate history. Then, just when things seemed to be going his way, Johnson's career and his life were threatened. In July 1955, he suffered a severe heart attack, and there were doubts that he would be able to continue his strenuous schedule as majority leader.

Johnson had always known that men in his family were plagued by heart disease. Perhaps this was one of the reasons he always seemed to be "in a great,

Johnson and Lady Bird at their Texas ranch in 1955, when Johnson was recuperating from his first serious heart attack.

great hurry," as a colleague in the House once put it. Now, he was grounded. For the last six months of 1955, he recuperated in Texas with Lady Bird and their daughters, who were now eight and eleven years old. Still strongly attached to the Texas Hill Country, Johnson and Lady Bird had already begun to buy land along the Pedernales River. Over the next 20 years, the Johnsons planned and built their ranch, which became their refuge from Washington.

When the Senate met in January 1956, Johnson returned, healthy and fit. He intensified his efforts to build bridges to all factions in the party. He continued to work with Senator Russell and the Southern conservatives, but also reached out to the leaders of the Northern liberals, including Minnesota senator Hubert Humphrey. He began to see himself as a leader who could pass important legislation by promoting compromise, both within his own party and with the Republican administration.

The Civil Rights Act

In 1956 President Eisenhower was re-elected, but the Democrats kept a narrow majority in the Senate. When the new Congress convened in January 1957, the most pressing issue facing the nation was civil rights for African Americans. The month before, Rosa Parks, an African American woman in Montgomery, Alabama, refused to give up her seat in the "whites only" section of a local bus. She was removed from the bus and arrested. Soon a young African American pastor, the Reverend Martin Luther King Jr., was helping blacks organize a *boycott* in Montgomery, refusing to ride the buses or buy goods at local businesses until segregation laws were changed.

That summer the Eisenhower administration submitted a bill to Congress strengthening federal protection of civil rights. Johnson, who had dodged civil rights issues for years, prepared to meet the challenge. He realized that the time for new government action on civil rights had come, and he resolved to work with the administration to move the new bill through the Senate. He knew that success could help make him a political leader with a national following, but he also believed deeply that minorities deserved equal treatment. Years later he told biographer Doris Kearns, "I wanted power to give things to people . . . especially the poor and the blacks."

Johnson was also a practical politician, and he understood the power of conservatives in the Senate. If the bill was too radical, the Southern bloc would defeat it, and no civil rights bill would pass. Johnson worked with liberals, urging them to concentrate on voting rights for African Americans, an issue that had broad national support. The new bill established a federal Civil Rights Commission and set up a new civil rights section in the Justice Department to monitor voting in the South. Southern senators insisted on an amendment that weakened the act by leaving voting rights enforcement in the hands of local authorities. Johnson persuaded supporters of the bill to accept the amendment. At the same time, he warned the conservatives that if the compromise amendment passed, they must not obstruct passage of the whole act. Photos of Johnson show him engaged in his consensus-building "treatment"—holding a senator's suit lapel with one hand, his face only inches from the senator's, his other hand jabbing a finger into the senator's chest as he made his point.

 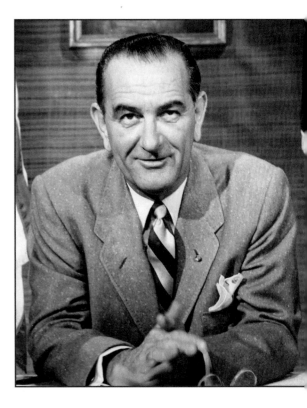

Republican president Dwight Eisenhower (left) was a widely popular president. Democratic Senate leader Lyndon Johnson (right) worked with the Eisenhower administration in 1957 to pass civil rights legislation.

In the end, Johnson succeeded in passing the bill in the Senate. President Eisenhower signed it into law on September 9, 1957. Johnson was recognized as one of the architects of the bill, the first civil rights bill passed since 1875. Yet he was bombarded with criticism from both sides. Civil rights advocates weren't happy that the final bill had been weakened, leaving enforcement of voting rights to Southern juries. Southerners complained bitterly that the bill extended federal power and reduced the right of states to determine their own voting regulations. Yet observers agreed that Johnson had accomplished a huge feat getting any civil rights bill past the Senate's powerful conservatives.

Vice President ————————————————

Still in a hurry, Johnson set his sights on the presidency in 1960. He announced his candidacy and gathered delegate support for the Democratic National Convention, but others were ahead of him. The leading candidate was one of Johnson's Senate colleagues, John F. Kennedy of Massachusetts. Handsome and charming, Kennedy won crucial primaries and won the presidential nomination easily on the first ballot.

One of Kennedy's most serious weaknesses in the presidential race was his religion. No Roman Catholic had ever been elected president, and it seemed that Kennedy might run poorly in predominantly Protestant regions in the South and Midwest. To counter this weakness, it seemed logical that he would choose a Southerner to run for vice president. Lyndon Johnson was an obvious choice, but he was strongly opposed by Kennedy's brother and close adviser, Robert Kennedy. In the end, however, John Kennedy offered the vice-presidential nomination to Lyndon Johnson. Johnson knew that he would have little power and authority as vice president, but he was ready for a new challenge.

Johnson confers with presidential nominee John F. Kennedy during the 1960 Democratic convention. Johnson accepted Kennedy's invitation to become the nominee for vice president.

In the campaign Johnson stressed Democratic civil rights accomplishments in Congress. He likened Kennedy to earlier Democratic heroes like Franklin Roosevelt, and he spoke out against religious bigotry. The Democrats were running against Republican nominee Richard Nixon, then Eisenhower's vice president. The first televised debate between presidential candidates gave Kennedy a big boost, showing him as calm and charming and Nixon as nervous and ill at ease. The November race was extremely close. Of nearly 69 million votes cast, Kennedy had 49.7 percent, to Nixon's 49.6 percent. Kennedy would be the new president, and Lyndon Johnson the vice president.

Johnson soon learned how powerless the vice presidency was. His only Constitutional duty was to preside over the Senate, without being able to speak on the issues or to cast a vote (unless the Senate was tied). President Kennedy invited him to attend cabinet meetings, and he went on good will tours, but there was little chance to accomplish anything on his own. Even worse, Johnson felt out of place among Kennedy's advisers, many of whom had attended the best colleges and had known each other for years. Most of the time, Johnson remained silent. "I detested every minute of it," Johnson later told a biographer. Johnson's family, however, was happy with his more relaxed schedule.

Kennedy was the youngest person ever elected president, and he brought a sense of youth and adventure to the White House. His glamorous wife Jackie and their two small children captivated Americans. Kennedy challenged younger Americans to get involved in public service and become active in politics, bringing many new members to the Democratic party.

Despite his popularity, Kennedy was soon involved in serious difficulties. Not long after he took office, he approved an invasion of the island nation of Cuba, 90 miles (145 km) off the Florida coast, in the hope of overthrowing its leader, Fidel Castro, who was making alliances with the Soviet Union and other Communist nations. The 1,500 invaders were Cuban refugees who had fled Cuba when Castro took power, but they had been trained and equipped by the United States. The invasion was a disaster. More than a thousand exiles were captured, and Kennedy was forced to acknowledge that the failed operation was sponsored by the U.S. government.

Eighteen months later, in the fall of 1962, U.S. planes spotted a missile site in Cuba which included Soviet nuclear missiles that could easily reach U.S. cities. Kennedy announced the discovery publicly and ordered U.S. Navy ships to keep Soviet ships with military supplies from landing in Cuba. The world watched anxiously as Soviet ships approached the U.S. blockade. On October 24, the ships turned around and sailed away. A few days later, Soviet premier Nikita Khrushchev agreed to remove the missile sites. Kennedy's cool management of the crisis made it his finest hour as president.

In February 1963, Kennedy submitted a civil rights bill to Congress. Soon afterward, television news cameras captured images of demonstrating African Americans in Birmingham, Alabama, being driven back by water from powerful fire hoses and menacing police dogs. The grim scenes persuaded many Americans that stronger civil rights protections were needed. Encouraged by Kennedy's proposal, hundreds of thousands of civil rights supporters assembled in Washington that summer. There Martin Luther King Jr. expressed the hopes of African Americans in his famous "I have a Dream" speech.

Tragedy ———————————————————

In November, President Kennedy planned a trip to Texas to help mend disputes between conservative and liberal Democrats there. Leading Democrats warned that he would be met by ugly demonstrations. "Well, that makes it more interesting," Kennedy replied. On November 22, 1963, *Air Force One*, the presidential jet, landed in Dallas. Kennedy was accompanied by his wife and Vice President Johnson. They were met by Texas governor John Connally.

Just after noon, Kennedy was riding in a motorcade through Dallas when shots suddenly rang out. The president was mortally wounded, and Governor Connally, riding in the same car, was injured. Lyndon Johnson was only two cars behind Kennedy's. Kennedy died soon afterward at a nearby hospital.

Johnson decided to return to Washington, D.C., immediately, carrying Kennedy's casket aboard *Air Force One*. Before the plane left the ground, Johnson was sworn in as president on the plane, with the slain president's widow Jacqueline beside him, her face swollen from weeping. When the jet landed at

November 22, 1963, hours after the death of President Kennedy, Johnson is sworn in as president on *Air Force One* at the Dallas airport. Lady Bird is at the left, and Jacqueline Kennedy, the slain president's widow, is at the right.

Andrews Air Force Base near Washington, he read a short statement, which ended with these words: "I know that the world shares the sorrow that Mrs. Kennedy and her family bear. I will do my best. This is all I can do. I ask for your help— and God's."

Chapter 4

Honoring Kennedy's Memory ————

As the nation mourned the loss of the slain president, Johnson prepared to take the reins of government. In a televised speech he asked Congress to pass legislation important to Kennedy, including a civil rights bill currently stalled in House committees. Johnson believed that Kennedy had been too easygoing in dealing with Congress, and he meant to change that. He knew the public expected him to carry on Kennedy's policies, but he wanted to put his own stamp on the office he'd unexpectedly inherited. He believed he had the skills to put new programs in place.

Over the Christmas holidays, Johnson announced from his ranch that his budget for 1964 would include an anti-poverty program. He set his staff members to work researching and suggesting program possibilities. Johnson also wanted to honor Kennedy's plan to cut taxes. The Senate warned that a tax cut and new social programs weren't both possible. Johnson responded by finding cuts in the federal budget, even trimming the White House electric bill.

He first showed Congress his presidential muscle when he sent military planes out to bring members, who were at home for the 1963 Christmas holidays, back to Washington to approve a sale of wheat to the Soviet Union that Kennedy had pushed for. Then Johnson was ready to tackle the always-controversial subject of civil rights. Polls showed that most Americans were ready to embrace stronger civil rights protections, and Johnson believed that racist policies in the South were holding that region back.

At the time, African Americans were not welcome in many restaurants, hotels, or sports stadiums. In theaters they were required to sit in special "Negroes only" sections. The proposed civil rights bill called for an end to segregation in all public accommodations and gave the *federal government* (the national government in Washington) power to enforce the law. The act also strengthened federal enforcement of voting laws, desegregation of public schools, and equal opportunity in hiring.

Johnson employed a rarely used rule to pull the bill out of a House committee and onto the floor for debate. Once it passed the House and headed to the Senate for approval, Johnson worked on the Southern senators. He called them at

President Johnson shakes hands with civil rights leader Martin Luther King Jr. after signing the landmark Civil Rights Act of 1964.

home and, if they weren't there, talked to their wives or children about the bill's importance: "Now you tell your daddy that the president called and he'd be very proud to have your daddy on his side."

Under pressure from the new president and from civil rights leaders in every part of the country, the Senate finally passed the bill and Johnson signed it on July 2, 1964. The Civil Rights Act of 1964 was a huge step beyond the 1957 act, and it remains one of Johnson's great achievements. Even before the Civil Rights Act was passed, Johnson was at work on his next great initiative. In May 1964, he unveiled plans for the program that he called the "Great Society," which would seek to address the roots of poverty in America.

War on the Horizon

That summer Johnson was also facing momentous decisions overseas. In 1954, ten years earlier, France had withdrawn from its former colony of Vietnam after a costly war with insurgent Vietnamese. The country was divided between Communist-led North Vietnam, supported by the Soviet Union, and South Vietnam, which received assistance from France and the United States. Beginning in 1959, Communist guerrilla fighters in the South, supported by North Vietnam, began to attack government positions there. Presidents Eisenhower and Kennedy sent military advisers to help the South Vietnamese army, but the fighting continued. By

1964, the South was in danger of being taken over by the guerrillas, known as the Vietcong.

President Johnson felt a responsibility to keep commitments to non-Communist South Vietnam, and he believed that if it fell to the Communists, other nations in Southeast Asia would also be threatened. Then in August 1964, North Vietnamese forces attacked the U.S. destroyer *Maddox* in the Gulf of Tonkin. In response, Johnson asked Congress to pass a resolution giving him the power to conduct further military actions in Vietnam. Congress passed the Gulf of Tonkin Resolution, and the war became Johnson's responsibility. The growing conflict there would come to haunt his presidency.

President in His Own Right ——————

Meanwhile, Johnson was preparing to run for a full term as president in 1964. He was easily nominated for president and chose liberal Minnesota senator Hubert Humphrey as his running mate. Johnson had seen too many close elections. This time he was aiming for the biggest landslide in the history of presidential elections. The Republican party helped him by nominating one of its most conservative leaders, Arizona senator Barry Goldwater. Goldwater was a fierce anti-Communist who favored a combative foreign policy. In one statement, he expressed the belief that nuclear weapons could provide "just enough firepower to get the job done."

At left, Republican presidential candidate Barry Goldwater of Arizona waves to supporters during a rodeo parade in his home state. Above, Democratic candidate Lyndon Johnson waves his Texas hat to supporters at a campaign rally. This was the first time both major presidential candidates came from the Southwest.

The Johnson campaign played on voters' fears about Goldwater's views, and he won re-election with 61 percent of the vote, the highest percentage in any presidential election up to that time. Democrats also won large majorities in both houses of Congress.

Johnson's 1965 State of the Union address presented ambitious plans for America, including initiatives in education, health care, the environment, and the arts. Johnson felt his usual sense of urgency, hoping to enact his programs while he had broad support and majorities in Congress. Soon after the address, Congress received Johnson's Medicare proposal, which would provide health care for retired Americans. A few days later he submitted a $1.5 billion education proposal.

To woo leaders of the 89th Congress, which first met in January, Johnson held White House breakfast feasts at which he encouraged and nagged House and Senate chiefs to move his proposals through Congress. "You treat them as if they were the president," he instructed his staff.

By the fall of 1965, Congress had passed the Medicare act and a major education act. It also created the Department of Housing and Urban Development and the National Endowment for the Arts. Johnson leaned especially hard on passage of educational projects because he believed that education offered one sure

Lady Bird Johnson visits a Head Start classroom in Washington, D.C. Head Start provides prekindergarten classes and activities for needy children.

way for the poor to better themselves. The Head Start program, providing pre-school classes for children from low-income families, was approved earlier and served more than 500,000 children that summer.

In March 1965, Martin Luther King Jr. led a march for voter registration through Alabama. State troopers stopped the marchers in a remote area and refused to let them continue. Demonstrators were beaten and sprayed with tear gas. Once again, television brought the ugly event to viewers across the country. In response, President Johnson sent a new proposal to Congress to outlaw the roadblocks that Southern communities and states put in the way of African Americans wanting to vote. It would prohibit literacy tests (usually administered only to black applicants) and poll taxes in voting registration. Again Johnson worked vigorously to persuade Southern senators to pass the bill. They responded, and Johnson signed the Voting Rights Act of 1965 on August 6. At the bill-signing ceremony, he urged African Americans to use the new law: "You must register. You must vote. . . . Your future, and your children's future, depend on it."

Riots and Protest

There was little time to celebrate the voting rights victory. On August 11 in Watts, a large African American neighborhood in Los Angeles, a routine traffic arrest set off six days of bloody and destructive riots. More than 30 people were killed, hundreds were injured, and 4,000 were taken into custody. Damage, mainly to white-owned businesses, added up to more than a billion dollars. Watts residents were angry about their treatment at the hands of the largely white Los Angeles police force and about much more—high unemployment, discrimination in housing and hiring, and lack of hope for a better future. Up to this time, the civil rights movement had concentrated on equality of African Americans in the South. Now Northern cities would see more violent protests in their own African American communities.

That fall, other demonstrations and protests were mounted against the growing American involvement in Vietnam. In February, Johnson had begun bombing raids on military sites in North Vietnam. In March 1965, the first 3,500 American combat troops landed in South Vietnam. Johnson was under growing pressure from the commander of U.S. military operations in Vietnam, General William Westmoreland, who urged the president to commit more troops and to step up the bombing of North Vietnam. Both were needed, he said, to destroy the Vietcong and allow South Vietnam to set up a democratic government.

Building the Great Society ────────────

As 1965 ended, the U.S. economy was in good shape, and most Americans still approved of Johnson's handling of Vietnam. Johnson tried to direct public attention away from Vietnam toward another "war," his war on poverty. In his January 1966 State of the Union address, he presented the results of research conducted by his staff that outlined needs for job training, housing, and education to help poor people rise out of poverty.

LBJ and the Telephone

One demand that Johnson placed on his staff was that they be available at all times. That meant taking little or no vacation time and having telephones installed even in home bathrooms. Johnson used the telephone as his main contact with aides, advisers, supporters, and opponents. An artist commissioned to sculpt his image couldn't get Johnson to stay off the telephone while she worked, so she made the phone a part of her sculpture.

President Johnson spent untold hours on the telephone, reaching out to supporters and opponents alike to help pass his administration's programs.

☆ ☆ ☆

Johnson's work habits hadn't changed; he still labored well into the night, sometimes past midnight, on a regular basis. He still expected a similar attitude from his staff. In spite of his hard-driving style, Johnson won the admiration of many who worked with him. Secretary of Defense Robert McNamara told Joseph

Califano, who was about to go to work for the president, "You will never work for a more complicated man as long as you live. But you're also not likely to work for a more intelligent one."

Working for Johnson was a mixed blessing; Johnson might berate a staff member one day, and present him with an expensive gift the next. Long workdays were punctuated with hilarious stories and jokes from a president who could be downright "zany." Yet Johnson could also be moody and emotional, and was especially irritable when Lady Bird was out of town. Johnson was often rude to his wife in public, but she was an important anchor in his life.

In 1966 Congress again went into a legislative fever, handling bills from the White House dealing with free school lunches for poor children, tougher air pollution laws, a new Department of Transportation, and something the president was particularly excited about: the Model Cities program. Model Cities aimed to rebuild chosen inner-city neighborhoods across America and improve poor residents' access to health care, job training, and better schools. In this case, though, Congress slashed the budget to the bone, and the program never had the impact Johnson had hoped for.

When the 89th Congress adjourned in October 1966, Johnson's accomplishments were "monumental," according to former aide Joseph Califano. Congress passed 84 bills originated by the president during 1965, and 97 more in

1966. In August 1965, a *New York Times* columnist commented that Johnson had accomplished in less than one year what many presidents do in two terms. Even so, Johnson often complained that his legislative achievements never received enough attention.

Vietnam Shadows

One reason for flagging attention to Johnson's accomplishments at home was bad news from the war. By the end of 1966 there were 385,000 U.S. troops in Vietnam, and 6,600 had died there. Johnson agonized over committing more and more young Americans to battle, and he was deeply troubled by reports of casualties. Yet the situation in Vietnam was not improving. Now North Vietnam was sending regular army troops into the South to fight alongside the guerrilla Vietcong and was receiving economic aid from the Soviet Union and China. As the cost of the war increased by billions of dollars, Johnson also realized that these new expenditures would soon cut into funds available for his ambitious programs at home.

To make matters worse, Johnson's advisers began giving him conflicting advice. The "doves" urged him to stop bombing North Vietnam in the hope that it would be encouraged to talk peace. The "hawks" advised him to step up the

President Johnson greets U.S. troops in Vietnam with General William Westmoreland.

bombing and send more troops. More often than not, the hawks won the debate. Late in 1966, Robert McNamara admitted to Johnson that he'd been concealing the estimated cost of the war—$20 billion for the year beginning October 1, 1966—from the president and the public.

War protest rallies were becoming more frequent, and Johnson took them personally, as he did any kind of negative response to his actions. Protesters used harsh words. One of their chants was, "Hey, hey, LBJ, how many kids did you kill today?" News commentators, struggling to understand the changes in war strategy and vague budget figures, began talking about Johnson's "credibility gap." At the same time, Johnson struggled with the credibility gap in the military reports he received. Descriptions of progress on the ground in Vietnam often turned out to be more wishful thinking than real advances. Johnson summed up his own predicament when he admitted, "It's not doing what is right that's hard for a president. It's knowing what's right."

Chapter 5

The Tide Turns ——————————

The congressional elections in November 1966 were an early sign that Johnson's great legislative achievements were near an end. Democrats elected majorities to both the House and the Senate, but lost many seats. In the House, they lost 47 seats to Republicans. It was clear that conservatives in both parties would be more powerful in the new 90th Congress.

The president's other problem was Vietnam. As the war escalated, it turned attention away from new programs at home and cut off any new spending. Throughout his career he'd been the practical politician who found ways to advance his own career by passing needed legislation. Vietnam presented him with a situation where he might have to choose between his career and his duty as president.

U.S. planes dropped thousands of bombs on North Vietnamese military bases and cities in 1966.

Johnson did not give up hope, however. In his 1967 State of the Union address, he asked Congress to help expand Medicare and Social Security benefits, establish a Corporation for Public Broadcasting, and pass a Safe Streets Act to combat growing crime. He expressed resolve to stay in Vietnam, even though "we face more cost, more loss, and more agony" there. With that, he announced plans for a tax increase, but he would not be able to persuade Congress to pass the unpopular proposal.

As Congress debated these new and expanded programs, Johnson did manage some solid accomplishments. In April, the Fair Housing Act was introduced, prohibiting discrimination because of race or ethnic origin in selling or renting a home. The president also nominated Thurgood Marshall to the Supreme Court, who would become the first African American to serve on the court. Marshall had been a leading lawyer in *Brown* v. *Board of Education*, the 1954 case in which the U.S. Supreme Court declared that segregated public schools were unconstitutional.

Staying the Course in Vietnam

There was little good news from Vietnam. For the first time, television news reporters brought video cameras right to the battlefields, and viewers at home saw images of the fearful war up close and in color. Anti-war demonstrations continued to spread, and some young men subject to the draft sought to avoid fighting by declaring themselves *conscientious objectors*, opposed to all wars, or fled to Canada to avoid being drafted into the military service.

Johnson pursued the war on many levels. Publicly, he remained firm, urging Americans to stay the course and continue to meet the country's commitments abroad, however painful that might be. In private, he searched for a way to negotiate a reasonable settlement—one that would allow South Vietnam a chance to establish a non-Communist government. The North Vietnamese and the Vietcong were not interested in peace proposals. They sensed that they could outlast Americans' will to stay and fight in Vietnam. Many South Vietnamese sympathized with the Vietcong, whose "hit-and-run" tactics allowed them to attack and withdraw without suffering huge losses. American and South Vietnamese troops were much better equipped, but their heavy weapons were of little use against an enemy that could fade into the countryside.

Anti-war views had spread from college campuses to larger groups of protesters and citizens. Large rallies were held in major cities, and anti-war demonstrations became a daily occurrence in Washington. Members of Congress began to ask more critical questions about the war. A leading critic was Robert Kennedy, the brother of the slain president, who had been elected to the Senate from New

Huge crowds march on U.S. military headquarters at the Pentagon (right) in 1967 to urge an end to the war in Vietnam. One sign identifies President Johnson as a "war criminal."

Lyndon Johnson's complex personality also included a sharp wit. When asked if he played favorites with his staff, he said, "There are no favorites in my office. I treat them all with the same general inconsideration."

As the press grew more critical of his performance, Johnson commented with a combination of irritation and humor, "If one morning I walked on top of the water across the Potomac River, the headline that afternoon would read 'President Can't Swim.'"

☆★☆

York in 1964. Even within the administration, Johnson's advisers began expressing doubts about continually enlarging the war. Secretary of Defense McNamara, long a pro-war "hawk," became more and more discouraged with the results of the war. In November 1967 he resigned.

By the end of 1967, Johnson had added the Air Quality Act and creation of the Corporation for Public Broadcasting to his list of achievements; he was named "Man of the Year" by *Time* magazine. Both of the Johnson daughters were married now, and Johnson often played in the Oval Office with his baby grandson. Privately, he considered not running for re-election in 1968, encouraged by Lady Bird, who hoped for a less stressful retirement with her husband.

Bowing Out

In his State of the Union address in January 1968, Johnson proposed more new initiatives to Congress including new programs to increase jobs and housing. He also announced that he would try again to increase taxes to reduce the growing budget *deficit* (the amount by which a government spends more in a year than it takes in). Johnson also expressed his hope for peace in Vietnam, even as more American troops were scheduled to join the 500,000 already there.

Later that month the war took a turn for the worse. On January 30, at the beginning of Tet, the Vietnamese new year celebration, Vietcong and North Vietnamese troops launched a major offensive, attacking more than 100 towns and villages. Some units reached the outskirts of Saigon, the South's capital city, shelling the U.S. Embassy and other targets. U.S. and South Vietnamese troops responded effectively, and the attackers retreated once more to their bases in the countryside. Still, the offensive illustrated that Communist forces remained strong and determined.

The Tet offensive triggered deep discouragement in the United States. By March, only 26 percent of Americans approved Johnson's handling of the war. Even Walter Cronkite, the widely respected anchorman of CBS News,

Who: The Vietcong (guerrilla fighters in South Vietnam) and the Communist government of North Vietnam; non-Communist South Vietnam with heavy support from the United States.

Where: South Vietnam, neighboring Cambodia and Laos; North Vietnam was heavily bombed by U.S. air forces

Why: Communist North Vietnam and non-Communist South Vietnam could not agree on unified government; in 1950s, Communist guerillas sought to overthrow South Vietnamese government and unify the country by force. The U.S. came to the defense of South Vietnam.

When: U.S. sent first troops in early 1960s, combat troops in 1965; by 1968, 550,000 were committed. Troop strength gradually reduced after 1969; armistice in January 1973 brought cease-fire and ended U.S. involvement.

Outcome: In 1975, after U.S. withdrawal, North Vietnamese forces overran the South; South Vietnam's government collapsed and Vietnam was united under a single Communist government.

observed that the United States was making no progress in Vietnam. "If I've lost Cronkite, I've lost middle America," Johnson said.

Opposition to the war was also affecting presidential politics. In late 1967, Senator Eugene McCarthy of Minnesota announced that he would run for the Democratic nomination for president in 1968 as a peace candidate. In the New Hampshire primary in February, he ran a close second to Johnson, with 42 percent of the vote to Johnson's 50 percent. Soon afterward, Senator Robert Kennedy announced his own peace candidacy. Governor George Wallace of Alabama, who opposed Johnson's civil rights and Great Society programs, also decided to run, rallying conservative Southern Democrats to his cause.

Exhausted and discouraged, Johnson reviews his address to the nation on March 31, 1968. He announced that he would not run for another term as president.

On March 31, President Johnson addressed the nation, outlining a new initiative to begin peace talks to end the war. He urged citizens to stand behind the government and to resist further division. Then, at the end of his long address, he surprised the nation and most of his advisers by announcing that he would drop out of the presidential race:

> With America's sons in the fields far away, with America's future under challenge right here at home, with our hopes and the world's hopes for peace in the balance every day, I do not believe that I should devote an hour or a day of my time to any personal partisan causes or to any duties other than the awesome duties of this office—the presidency of your country.
>
> Accordingly, I shall not seek, and I will not accept, the nomination of my party for another term as your president.

Response to the announcement was positive. The *Washington Post* praised Johnson's decision to "put unity ahead of his own advancement and . . . pride." Soon afterward, Congress passed a tax increase, and North Vietnam expressed willingness begin peace talks.

Deepening Distress ————————

Johnson's surprise announcement was soon lost in a new round of shock and dismay. Only five days later, on April 4, civil rights leader Martin Luther King Jr. was assassinated in Memphis, Tennessee. African American activist Stokely Carmichael declared that the murder of King amounted to a declaration of war by "white America" against blacks. Once again, riots broke out in Washington, D.C., and other cities. Johnson hoped to attend the funeral for King in Atlanta, but was prevented by death threats. At the president's urging, however, Congress did pass the Fair Housing Act, prohibiting racial discrimination in selling or renting homes, as a tribute to Dr. King. The bill had been held up in Congress for nearly a year.

At the end of April, Vice President Hubert Humphrey announced that he would seek the Democratic nomination for president. Johnson certainly preferred his vice president to the peace Democrats, and he knew that Humphrey had served loyally as vice president. Yet he refused to offer any public support for Humphrey's campaign before the Democratic convention in August.

The political scene changed once again in June. Senator Kennedy won the important presidential primary in California on June 5, becoming a favorite to win the Democratic nomination. Moments after making his victory statement, however, he was shot and killed by an assassin. Kennedy and Johnson had never

In the spring of 1968, civil rights leader Martin Luther King Jr. (left) and anti-war presidential candidate Robert F. Kennedy (right) were both assassinated. Their deaths caused renewed racial violence and helped divide the Democratic party.

been friendly, and the president had resented Kennedy's criticisms of his administration, but he was shocked by Kennedy's death. "There are no words to equal the horror of this tragedy," he said.

In August the Democratic convention met in Chicago to nominate candidates for president and vice president. Outside the convention hall, thousands of anti-war demonstrators gathered to protest the continuing war. In violent clashes with Chicago police, dozens were injured and others were arrested and charged with crimes. Television images of this new violence crowded out the story of the convention, which nominated Hubert Humphrey for president. To avoid the angry demonstrations, Johnson had stayed away from the convention, spending the week at his Texas ranch.

Earlier that summer, the Republicans had nominated Richard Nixon as their presidential candidate. The former vice president had lost the 1960 presidential election to John F. Kennedy. Now he promised to bring the nation together, to achieve "peace with honor" in Vietnam, and to establish "law and order" to end violence in the nation's cities.

Defeat

Johnson still hoped to be able bring an end to the war in Vietnam before leaving office in January 1969. Peace talks with all sides in Vietnam were going well.

Hopes for peace were dashed, however—not by the Vietcong or the North Vietnamese, but by the refusal of South Vietnam's government to join the talks. There were dark rumors that Republican supporters encouraged the South Vietnamese to stall to help gain Nixon's election, but the rumors were not reported during the campaign and were never proved. On election day, Nixon won the presidency with 43.2 percent of the vote to Humphrey's 42.7 percent and George Wallace's 13.6 percent.

During his last few weeks in office, Johnson went on a campaign to preserve natural wonders. By executive order he created new parks, scenic trails, and wilderness areas. Lady Bird, a longtime supporter of wilderness protection and highway beautification, dedicated a park named for her on an island in the Potomac River.

In his last State of the Union address to Congress, Johnson proudly summed up his five years in office and expressed sadness at not having been able to end the war in Vietnam. "Now, it is time to leave. I hope it may be said . . . that by working together we helped to make our country more just." Johnson was cheered and applauded, and tearful members of Congress sang "Auld Lang Syne" as he left the congressional chamber.

On January 20, 1969, after Nixon's inauguration, the Johnsons went to Andrews Air Force Base to fly home to Texas. Among the crowd gathered to see

Outgoing president Johnson shakes hands with incoming president Richard Nixon at Nixon's inauguration in January 1969.

them off was Texas Republican congressman George Bush. Bush said he came to Johnson's farewell because "he has been a fine president [and I wanted] to show in a small way how much I have appreciated him." Bush, who would later become the 41st president, represented the political future of Texas. After decades of domination by Democrats, the state would soon become a Republican stronghold.

Chapter 6

A Difficult Transition ————————————

Johnson was exhausted by his years of 16- to 18-hour days as president. His first order of business was a long rest. He avoided reporters, declaring, "I've served my time with that bunch." He relished the chance "to spend a little more time with my kin folks." As president, he had taken his health seriously, giving up smoking and drinking and watching his weight. Now that he could relax, he resumed his lax habits. He ate what he wanted and made frequent visits to his favorite hamburger joint in Austin. He put on weight and let his hair grow down to his shoulders. "If I want to have some bad manners, I'm going to have bad manners," he said. "I've got to have some freedom to do what I want to do."

Still, leisure time was a struggle for Johnson. Away from the center of power in Washington, he became depressed at first. Lady

Lyndon Johnson in retirement at his ranch in Texas.

Bird invited old friends to the ranch, but he still seemed gloomy. In July 1969, President Nixon invited the Johnsons to the launching of *Apollo 11*, on its way to the moon. Johnson later remembered it as an event at which he felt very unimportant, even though he had been greeted warmly and was seated next to the new vice president, Spiro Agnew.

With time, he adjusted to his new life on the ranch, finding much to enjoy. The Johnsons received a comfortable government pension and owned profitable businesses. Johnson paid loving attention to his wife, who had patiently endured an often-hurtful marriage, and played for hours at a time with his grandchildren.

The Lyndon Johnson National Historical Park

While he was working on his ranch, LBJ envisioned his "Texas White House" as a future park. Today it is a part of a national historical park, managed by the National Park Service. It continues as a working ranch, using the ranching techniques Johnson favored in the 1970s. Visitors can observe the ranch hands at work and experience the robust beauty of the Texas Hill Country, with its breezy fields of tall grass, vivid wildflowers, and stands of live oak trees. Nearby is the schoolhouse that Johnson entered at the age of four. Another section of the park is located in Johnson City, about 15 miles (24 km) east of the ranch. There visitors can see Johnson's boyhood home. Special events at the park include a Ranch Roundup each April. On Johnson's birthday each August 27, family members gather at the cemetery where he is buried for a wreath-laying ceremony.

☆ ★ ☆

He devoted much of his energy to running his ranch just as he would have run a political campaign. One visiting friend, hoping to talk politics, was disappointed to find LBJ "only talks hog prices." In the White House, Johnson read hundreds of reports on political and military matters. Now his nightly reading included reports on how many eggs his prize hens were laying.

Keeping in Touch ───────────────────

Johnson kept up a friendly relationship with Richard Nixon, who occasionally called Johnson for advice and invited him to the White House. In public comments, Johnson urged Americans to support the president as he sought to end the war in Vietnam.

Another of Johnson's projects was helping to set up his presidential library and museum, which was located on the campus of the University of Texas in Austin, about 75 miles (120 km) from the ranch. It houses many of the documents produced during his administration and includes a replica of the Oval Office in the White House, which Johnson used when he was in Austin. He also worked with a group of writers and advisers on his memoirs, but he died before they were finished.

Even in retirement, Johnson showed flashes of his old ability to build bridges between opposing groups to achieve a higher goal. During a civil rights discussion at the Johnson Library in December 1972, arguments broke out between conservative and radical civil rights leaders. Johnson took the stage. "Until every boy and girl born into this land . . . can stand on the same level ground, our job will not be done," Johnson told the cheering crowd. Then he urged them to patch up their differences and unite in their common goals, which would strengthen their message and impact.

Final Days

The civil rights meeting was one of Johnson's last public appearances. For several years he had been suffering chest pains, signs of the heart disease that had troubled him since the 1950s. On January 22, 1973, Johnson was alone at the ranch when he suffered a fatal heart attack. Secret Service agents tried to revive him but were unsuccessful. Johnson was flown by private plane to a hospital in San Antonio, but was pronounced dead on arrival.

His body lay in state at the LBJ Library in Austin and then in the Capitol Rotunda in Washington. Ironically, on the day Johnson died, President Nixon announced that an armistice had been signed, ending U.S. involvement in Vietnam. Had Johnson heard the good news? Reporters speculated that he hadn't, but Lady Bird assured them otherwise. "Fate was kind," she reported. "Lyndon did know that peace had come."

Johnson's Legacy

Lyndon Johnson served during tumultuous times and was a target of heated criticism while in office. For many years, his accomplishments seemed overshadowed by the Vietnam War, which had divided Americans and called into question Johnson's abilities as president. His roles in increasing U.S. involvement and in setting military strategy are still debated, hawks claiming that he was not resolute enough to win the war and doves claiming that he was too harsh and inflexible.

Johnson's presidency was also attacked by leaders who disputed his belief that social problems are best addressed by the federal government. In the 1980s, President Ronald Reagan argued that big government was not a solution to social ills—big government was the problem. Since Johnson's presidency, reforms have limited government spending for welfare and for many of Johnson's Great Society programs. Since Johnson's time, presidents have avoided large new federal programs, seeking to give more problem-solving responsibility to local and state governments.

Even after all these criticisms of Johnson, historians have given him high marks as president. In recent polls of American historians, Johnson ranks among the top 12 or 15 U.S. presidents. He gets especially high marks for his ability to get his ambitious programs passed by Congress. Few presidents in

Lady Bird and Lyndon Johnson on the LBJ Ranch.

history have a better legislative record. More important, Johnson is credited with passing landmark civil rights legislation, protecting and enforcing the civil rights of African Americans and other minorities. As Johnson biographer Robert Caro writes, "Abraham Lincoln struck off the chains of black Americans, but it was Lyndon Johnson who led them into voting booths." Johnson also originated government programs that remain popular more than 40 years after their passage, including Medicare, which offers medical coverage for retired people, and Head Start, which provides preschool education for children from low-income homes.

Lyndon Johnson's presidency was a turning point in the country's history. As a champion of civil rights, he helped bring African Americans and other minorities into the mainstream of American life and brought the country closer to its ideals of equal rights and equal opportunity. At the same time, as president during a divisive and disputed war, he raised new questions about the role of the United States in the world which have still not been answered.

Fast Facts Lyndon Baines Johnson

Birth:	August 27, 1908
Birthplace:	Stonewall, Texas
Parents:	Sam Ealy Johnson Jr. and Rebekah Baines Johnson
Sisters & Brothers:	Rebekah (1910–1978)
	Josefa (1912–1961)
	Sam Houston (1914–1978)
	Lucia (1916–1997)
Education:	Southwest Texas State Teachers College, San Marcos, Texas; B.A., 1930
Occupations:	Teacher; congressional aide; federal program administrator
Marriage:	To Claudia (Lady Bird) Taylor, November 17, 1934
Children:	(see First Lady Fast Facts at right)
Political Party:	Democratic
Public Offices:	1937–1949 Member, U.S. House of Representatives
	1949–1961 U.S. Senator
	1961–1963 Vice President of the United States
	1963–1969 36th President of the United States
His Vice President:	Hubert H. Humphrey
Major Actions as President:	1964 Signed Civil Rights Act of 1964
	1964 Signed Gulf of Tonkin Resolution, beginning buildup of U.S. war effort in Vietnam
	1965 Began U.S. bombing of North Vietnam
	1965 Signed Voting Rights Act of 1965, Medicare Act
	1965 Head Start program for preschool children began
	1965 Established new Department of Housing and Urban Development
	1966 Established new Department of Transportation
	1968 Withdrew from presidential race, hoping to end war
Death:	January 22, 1973
Age at Death:	64
Burial Place:	Johnson family cemetery, near his birthplace

Fast Facts

Claudia (Lady Bird) Taylor Johnson

Birth:	December 22, 1912
Birthplace:	Karnack, Texas
Parents:	Thomas Jefferson Taylor and Minnie Pattillo Taylor
Brothers & Sisters:	Two older brothers
Education:	University of Texas, Austin; B.A., 1933; journalism degree, 1934
Marriage:	To Lyndon Baines Johnson, November 17, 1934
Children:	Lynda Bird Johnson (1944–)
	Luci Baines Johnson (1947–)
Firsts:	Helped develop and pass the Highway Beautification Act in 1965, which restricted billboards and junkyards along federally supported highways

Timeline

1908	1913	1927	1928	1930

1908
Lyndon Baines Johnson is born near Stonewall, Texas, August 27

1913
Moves with family to a farm near Johnson City, Texas

1927
Enters Southwest Texas State Teachers College in San Marcos

1928
Begins school year as teacher in impoverished Cotulla, Texas

1930
Graduates from Southwest Texas State; takes teaching job at Sam Houston High School in Houston

1947	1948	1954	1955	1957

1947
Daughter Luci Baines is born

1948
Johnson elected to U.S. Senate from Texas, by 87-vote margin; called "Landslide Lyndon"

1954
Re-elected to second six-year term in Senate

1955
Chosen Senate majority leader by Democratic senators

1957
Helps pass the Civil Rights Act of 1957

1965	1968	1968	1969	1971

1965
Begins bombing of North Vietnam; bombing campaign lasts three years

1968
Announces he won't run for re-election, March; Martin Luther King Jr. assassinated, April; Robert F. Kennedy killed, June

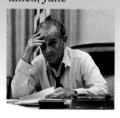

1968
Democrats nominate Hubert Humphrey for president, August; Republican Richard Nixon defeats Humphrey and wins presidency, November

1969
Johnson retires to LBJ Ranch in Texas

1971
Dedicates Lyndon Baines Johnson Library and Museum in Austin, Texas

1931	1934	1935	1937	1944

Becomes an assistant to Texas representative Richard Kleberg in Washington, D.C.

Marries Lady Bird Taylor, November 17

Appointed Texas director of the National Youth Administration, a federal youth employment program

Elected to U.S. House of Representatives from Texas's 10th District; re-elected 1938, 1940, 1942, 1944, 1946

Daughter Linda Bird is born

1960	1963	1964	1964	1965

Chosen Democratic vice-presidential candidate, July; elected vice president to serve under President John F. Kennedy, November

Kennedy assassinated November 22 in Dallas, Texas; Johnson sworn in as 36th president aboard presidential plane at Dallas airport

Signs Civil Rights Act of 1964; signs Gulf of Tonkin Resolution, beginning increased U.S. involvement in Vietnam War

Elected to full term as president by a landslide over Republican candidate Barry M. Goldwater

Signs bills establishing Head Start for preschool children and Medicare for elderly Americans

1973

Dies January 22 at LBJ Ranch in Texas

Glossary

bill: a proposed law or act presented to a legislature for debate and passage

boycott: an agreement by a group of people not to buy goods or services from businesses that have discriminated against them or caused other harm

censure: to condemn an elected official formally by vote of a legislative body

civil rights: the rights granted to all citizens in the U.S. Constitution, especially the right to equal treatment under the law

conscientious objector: a person who claims not to be subject to military service because of deep religious or moral objections to war

constituents: the people represented by an elected official

deficit: the amount by which a government spends more in a year than it takes in

federal government: the national government with headquarters in Washington, D.C.; used to distinguish it from state and local governments

lobby: an effort by representatives of businesses or organized groups to persuade legislators to pass legislation favorable to them

Further Reading

★ ★ ★ ★ ★

Kaye, Tony. *Lyndon B. Johnson*. New York: Chelsea House, 1988.

Levy, Debbie. *Lyndon B. Johnson*. Minneapolis: Lerner Publications, 2003.

Lindop, Edmund. *Dwight D. Eisenhower, John F. Kennedy, Lyndon B. Johnson*. New York: Twenty-First Century Books, 1997.

Schuman, Michael A. *Lyndon B. Johnson*. Springfield, NJ: Enslow, 1998.

MORE ADVANCED READING

Degregorio, William. *Complete Book of U.S. Presidents: From George Washington to Bill Clinton*. New York: Random House, 1997.

Goodwin, Doris Kearns. *Lyndon Johnson and the American Dream*. New York: Harper & Row, 1976.

Places to Visit

★ ★ ★ ★ ★

The United States Capitol

Capitol Hill

Washington, DC 20515

Visitor information: (202) 225-6827

The building where the U.S. House of Representatives and the U.S. Senate have met since 1800; Lyndon Johnson served in the House and Senate from 1937 to 1961.

Lyndon B. Johnson National Historical Park

P.O. Box 329

Johnson City, TX 78636

Visitor Information: (830) 868-7128 ext. 244

http://www.nps.gov/lyjo/

The park has two parts. The first is Johnson's boyhood home in Johnson City, about 60 miles (96 km) west of Austin, Texas. The second includes Johnson's birthplace and the "Texas White House" on the LBJ Ranch, about 15 miles (24 km) west of Johnson City.

The White House

1600 Pennsylvania Avenue NW

Washington, DC 20500

24-hour Visitors' Office Info Line: (202) 456-7041

Lyndon and Lady Bird Johnson lived here from 1964 until 1969.

Online Sites of Interest

★ **Internet Public Library, Presidents of the United States (IPL POTUS)**

http://www.potus.com/lbjohnson.html

Includes concise information about Johnson and his presidency and provides links to other sites of interest.

★ **American President.org**

www.americanpresident.org/history/lyndonbjohnson

Offers information about American presidents and the presidency, including a biography of Johnson and a timeline of his presidency.

★ **Grolier**

http://gi.grolier.com/presidents/

This site, sponsored by the publisher of reference materials, offers links to information about all the presidents. Material includes brief biographies at different reading levels, presidential portraits, and presidential election results.

★ **The White House**

www.whitehouse.gov/history/presidents

Offers brief biographical articles on each president and first lady.

★ **Lyndon B. Johnson National Historical Park**

http://www.nps.gov/lyjo/

★ **Lyndon Baines Johnson Library and Museum**

http://www.lbjlib.utexas.edu/

Provides useful information on the lives of Lyndon and Lady Bird Johnson, including special material for young readers.

Table of Presidents

	1. George Washington	**2. John Adams**	**3. Thomas Jefferson**	**4. James Madison**
Took office	Apr 30 1789	Mar 4 1797	Mar 4 1801	Mar 4 1809
Left office	Mar 3 1797	Mar 3 1801	Mar 3 1809	Mar 3 1817
Birthplace	Westmoreland Co, VA	Braintree, MA	Shadwell, VA	Port Conway, VA
Birth date	Feb 22 1732	Oct 20 1735	Apr 13 1743	Mar 16 1751
Death date	Dec 14 1799	July 4 1826	July 4 1826	June 28 1836

	9. William H. Harrison	**10. John Tyler**	**11. James K. Polk**	**12. Zachary Taylor**
Took office	Mar 4 1841	Apr 6 1841	Mar 4 1845	Mar 5 1849
Left office	**Apr 4 1841•**	Mar 3 1845	Mar 3 1849	**July 9 1850•**
Birthplace	Berkeley, VA	Greenway, VA	Mecklenburg Co, NC	Barboursville, VA
Birth date	Feb 9 1773	Mar 29 1790	Nov 2 1795	Nov 24 1784
Death date	Apr 4 1841	Jan 18 1862	June 15 1849	July 9 1850

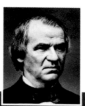   

	17. Andrew Johnson	**18. Ulysses S. Grant**	**19. Rutherford B. Hayes**	**20. James A. Garfield**
Took office	Apr 15 1865	Mar 4 1869	Mar 5 1877	Mar 4 1881
Left office	Mar 3 1869	Mar 3 1877	Mar 3 1881	**Sept 19 1881•**
Birthplace	Raleigh, NC	Point Pleasant, OH	Delaware, OH	Orange, OH
Birth date	Dec 29 1808	Apr 27 1822	Oct 4 1822	Nov 19 1831
Death date	July 31 1875	July 23 1885	Jan 17 1893	Sept 19 1881

5. James Monroe

Mar 4 1817

Mar 3 1825

Westmoreland Co, VA

Apr 28 1758

July 4 1831

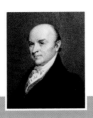

6. John Quincy Adams

Mar 4 1825

Mar 3 1829

Braintree, MA

July 11 1767

Feb 23 1848

7. Andrew Jackson

Mar 4 1829

Mar 3 1837

The Waxhaws, SC

Mar 15 1767

June 8 1845

8. Martin Van Buren

Mar 4 1837

Mar 3 1841

Kinderhook, NY

Dec 5 1782

July 24 1862

13. Millard Fillmore

July 9 1850

Mar 3 1853

Locke Township, NY

Jan 7 1800

Mar 8 1874

14. Franklin Pierce

Mar 4 1853

Mar 3 1857

Hillsborough, NH

Nov 23 1804

Oct 8 1869

15. James Buchanan

Mar 4 1857

Mar 3 1861

Cove Gap, PA

Apr 23 1791

June 1 1868

16. Abraham Lincoln

Mar 4 1861

Apr 15 1865•

Hardin Co, KY

Feb 12 1809

Apr 15 1865

21. Chester A. Arthur

Sept 19 1881

Mar 3 1885

Fairfield, VT

Oct 5 1829

Nov 18 1886

22. Grover Cleveland

Mar 4 1885

Mar 3 1889

Caldwell, NJ

Mar 18 1837

June 24 1908

23. Benjamin Harrison

Mar 4 1889

Mar 3 1893

North Bend, OH

Aug 20 1833

Mar 13 1901

24. Grover Cleveland

Mar 4 1893

Mar 3 1897

Caldwell, NJ

Mar 18 1837

June 24 1908

	25. William McKinley	**26. Theodore Roosevelt**	**27. William H. Taft**	**28. Woodrow Wilson**
Took office	Mar 4 1897	Sept 14 1901	Mar 4 1909	Mar 4 1913
Left office	**Sept 14 1901•**	Mar 3 1909	Mar 3 1913	Mar 3 1921
Birthplace	Niles, OH	New York, NY	Cincinnati, OH	Staunton, VA
Birth date	Jan 29 1843	Oct 27 1858	Sept 15 1857	Dec 28 1856
Death date	Sept 14 1901	Jan 6 1919	Mar 8 1930	Feb 3 1924

	33. Harry S. Truman	**34. Dwight D. Eisenhower**	**35. John F. Kennedy**	**36. Lyndon B. Johnson**
Took office	Apr 12 1945	Jan 20 1953	Jan 20 1961	Nov 22 1963
Left office	Jan 20 1953	Jan 20 1961	**Nov 22 1963•**	Jan 20 1969
Birthplace	Lamar, MO	Denison, TX	Brookline, MA	Johnson City, TX
Birth date	May 8 1884	Oct 14 1890	May 29 1917	Aug 27 1908
Death date	Dec 26 1972	Mar 28 1969	Nov 22 1963	Jan 22 1973

	41. George Bush	**42. Bill Clinton**	**43. George W. Bush**	
Took office	Jan 20 1989	Jan 20 1993	Jan 20 2001	
Left office	Jan 20 1993	Jan 20 2001	—	
Birthplace	Milton, MA	Hope, AR	New Haven, CT	
Birth date	June 12 1924	Aug 19 1946	July 6 1946	
Death date	—	—	—	

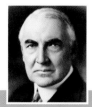

29. Warren G. Harding	30. Calvin Coolidge	31. Herbert Hoover	32. Franklin D. Roosevelt
Mar 4 1921	Aug 2 1923	Mar 4 1929	Mar 4 1933
Aug 2 1923•	Mar 3 1929	Mar 3 1933	**Apr 12 1945•**
Blooming Grove, OH	Plymouth, VT	West Branch, IA	Hyde Park, NY
Nov 21 1865	July 4 1872	Aug 10 1874	Jan 30 1882
Aug 2 1923	Jan 5 1933	Oct 20 1964	Apr 12 1945

37. Richard M. Nixon	38. Gerald R. Ford	39. Jimmy Carter	40. Ronald Reagan
Jan 20 1969	Aug 9 1974	Jan 20 1977	Jan 20 1981
Aug 9 1974★	Jan 20 1977	Jan 20 1981	Jan 20 1989
Yorba Linda, CA	Omaha, NE	Plains, GA	Tampico, IL
Jan 9 1913	July 14 1913	Oct 1 1924	Feb 6 1911
Apr 22 1994	——	——	June 5 2004

• Indicates the president died while in office.
★ Richard Nixon resigned before his term expired.

Index

Johnson, Lyndon B. (cont'd.)
family, 10, *13*, 30, 43, 74
fast facts, 96
and Great Society, 63-66
health, 23, 42-43, 87, 91
and Korean War, 39
legacy, 92, 94
marriage, 20, 21
and Medicare, 60
and National Youth Administration, 21-23
relationships with businessmen, 25-26
retirement, 87-91, *88*
and Senate campaign of 1941, 28
and Senate campaign of 1948, 33, 35-37, *36*
as Senator, 37-41, 42-44
as teacher, 13, 14, *14,* 15-16
and telephone, 64
timeline, 98-99
as vice president, 47-51
and Vietnam War, 56-57, 66-68, *67,* 82-83, 92
wartime service, 28-31, *29*
Johnson, Rebekah, 10, *11*
Johnson, Sam Ealy Jr., 10, 11, *11,* 12, 24
Johnson City, Texas, 23, 89
Johnson Library and Museum, 90, 91

Kennedy, John F., 47-51, *48,* 51, 56
Kennedy, Robert, 47, 72, 74, 76, 79, *81,* 82
Khrushchev, Nikita, 50
King, Martin Luther Jr., 44, 51, *55,* 62, 79, *80*
Kleberg, Richard, 16, 18, 19, 21
Korean War, 39, *40*

LBJ Ranch, *9,* 43, 89, 90, *93*
Lyndon Johnson National Historic Park, 89

Marshall, Thurgood, 71
McCarthy, Eugene, 76

McCarthy, Joseph, 41-42
McNamara, Robert, 64-65, 68, 74
Medicare, 60, 71, 94
Model Cities program, 65

National Endowment for the Arts, 60
National Youth Administration (NYA), 21-23, *22*
Naval Affairs Committee, 23
Navy, U.S., 29
New Deal, 18-19
Nixon, Richard, 48, 82, 83, *84,* 89, 90
North Atlantic Treaty Organization (NATO), 38
nuclear weapons, 57

O'Daniel, "Pappy," 28, 33, 35

poverty programs, 53-54, 63
protests, 8, 63, 68, 72, 82

Rayburn, Sam, 17-18, *18,* 21, *27, 32*
Republican party, 37, 48, 57, 69, 82
riots, 62-63, 79
Roosevelt, Franklin D., 18-19, 23, *24,* 26, 30-31, 48
Russell, Richard, 37, 39, 44

Safe Streets Act, 71
school lunch program, 14, 65
segregation, 54
Social Security, 71
Soviet Union, 31, 50, 54, 66
Stevenson, Coke, 35, 37
Supreme Court, U.S., 71

Taft-Hartley Act, 33
Taylor, Claudia. *See* Johnson, Lady Bird
telephone, 64

television, 42, 48-49, 62, 71, 82
Tet Offensive, 75
Transportation, Department of, 65
Truman, Harry, 31, *32,* 38, 39

Vietnam War, 56-57, 63, 66-68, *67*, 69-78, *70*, 92
  armistice, 91
  fast facts, 76
  opposition to, 8, *73*, 76
  peace talks, 82-83

Vietnam War (cont'd.)
  staying the course, 71-74
voting rights, 31, 37, 45, 46-47, 54, 62, 94
Voting Rights Act of 1965, 62

Wallace, George, 76, 83
war on poverty, 63
Watts, 62-63
Westmoreland, William, 63, *67*
World War II, 26, 28-31

About the Author

Jean Kinney Williams is a mother and a writer who lives in Ohio. She has written many books for young readers, including a series that tells about American religious groups such as the Amish and the Shakers.